Air Horns and F Bombs – The Alexa Experiment

By Rick Young

Table of Contents

Forward   3

Introduction   5

Chapter 1 – The Alexa Experiment   7

Chapter 2 - The Sprite Can Test   10

Chapter 3 - The Words You Do Not Say   14

Chapter 4 - The Two Words That Matter Most   19

Chapter 5 - The Lost Art of Saying No   22

Chapter 6 - The Art of Discipline   25

Chapter 7 - Know When to Let Go   28

Chapter 8 - The Greatest Gift – Confidence   32

Chapter 9 - Too Much, Too Soon   36

Chapter 10 - Pets, Playdough, and the Lie Your Kids Tell You   40

Chapter 11 - The Participation Trophy   45

Chapter 12 - The Disney Cruise   48

Chapter 13 - The Starburst Revolution	51
Chapter 14 - The Ring Doorbell Blockade	54
Chapter 15 - First Weekend Driving; Lies, Deception, and a Bent Bumper	57
Chapter 16 - Lessons in Metal and Grit	62
Chapter 17 - Flying Under the Radar is for Cowards	66
Chapter 18 - Lessons through Fireball	70
Chapter 19 - Leadership, Grit, and a Dirty Swimming Pool	74
Chapter 20 - Air Horns and F Bombs	79
Chapter 21 - Tough Love and Life Lessons	83
Chapter 22 - Choices Have Consequences, and That's a Damn Good Thing	87
Chapter 23 – Music & Mayhem	90
Chapter 24 – The Next Chapter	94
Conclusion	96

Foreword by Alexa Holibaugh

My name is Alexa Holibaugh. I'm the stepdaughter of Rick Young, the older sister to Sophie, and—like the title says—the experiment.

This is not your average parenting book. It doesn't beat around the bush—and neither did Rick. For some readers, it's going to be a hard dose of reality: the raw truth of raising a kid, lessons learned the hard way, and maybe, if you can get past the harsh delivery, some damn good advice on how to raise a tough, disciplined, real-world-ready kid.

For me? It didn't teach me how to be a parent. That's not what I needed.

What it gave me was something different: perspective.

Growing up, it's hard to understand why your parents are acting the way they do. They tell you it's "because they love you," but as a kid, that's impossible to really believe. I'd be lying if I said I understood it back then. I didn't. Like most kids, what was probably running through my head was something more like: *Screw you.*

But that changed—slowly—as I got older. And especially after reading this book.

Some of these stories, I was too young to remember. Others, I remember vividly—the situations and the emotions. But what I never knew back then was *why*. Why he did the things he did. What he was trying to teach me. (Okay, *except* for the JROTC leadership camp story—I was so exhausted I must've blacked out, but you'll read about that later.)

Here's my advice: read between the lines. Catch the messages and the lessons buried in the chaos, the yelling, and yes, the F-bombs. My stepdad is blunt. He's tough. And he's not going to sugarcoat a damn thing.

But if you can get past that, what you'll find is a brutally honest and unexpectedly loving guide to raising the first kid—the one who broke in the parent.

Enjoy.

—Alexa Holibaugh

Introduction

Let's get one thing straight right off the bat—this isn't a book for parents who tiptoe around their kids' feelings, hand out participation trophies, or think "consequences" is a dirty word, although they are the ones that should read this. If you're looking for a guide on how to validate every little emotion, negotiate bedtime like it's a UN peace treaty, or bubble-wrap your kid's self-esteem, you've picked up the wrong damn book.

Air Horns and F-Bombs is a guide for parents who believe in raising tough, capable, and independent kids—not fragile little "snowflakes" who melt the first time life doesn't go their way. The world isn't soft, and if you raise your kid to be, you're setting them up for a lifetime of failure, entitlement, and disappointment. I love my kids more than anything, and because I love them, I'm not going to coddle them. I'm going to prepare them.

There was a time when kids got their feelings hurt and learned to deal with it. They didn't need safe spaces or special accommodations for the harsh realities of life. They grew up knowing that hard work beats handouts, that respect isn't given—it's earned, and that no one gives a damn about your excuses. That's how I was raised, and that's how I raised my own kids. And guess what? The seem to be turning out just fine, although the jury might still be out.

This book is about bringing back *real* parenting—the kind that prioritizes discipline over comfort, respect over entitlement, and common sense over trendy nonsense. It's about setting boundaries, enforcing consequences, and teaching your kids how to navigate life without expecting the world to cater to their every whim.

So, if you're ready to parent like you mean it— without guilt, without second-guessing, and without raising a kid who falls apart when they hear the word "no"—then keep reading. You're in the right place. Let's get to work.

Chater 1 - The Alexa Experiment

Let's talk about firstborns. If you are the first kid in a household, I have some bad news for you: you are the experiment. The test subject. The prototype. Your parents are basically winging it, seeing what works, and what doesn't, and you, my dear child, are the unfortunate recipient of every first-time mistake. Congratulations, you get to be the family's crash-test dummy.

That brings us to Alexa—our oldest. Poor, poor Alexa. She had the distinct misfortune of being the first child through our household, meaning she didn't get the benefit of watching her older siblings screw up first. Nope, she got to pave that road herself, with all the bumps, bruises, and metaphorical potholes that come with it. And let me tell you, I was fully aware of this reality because I was the baby of my family. I watched my older sister and brother get into all sorts of trouble, and I learned. It was simple: just don't do what they did.

Did that make me an angel? Hell no. But my mother believed I was, and that, my friends, is called winning the war. I'm sure my father wasn't fooled, but my mother's rose-colored glasses worked in my favor. So in some ways, I was sympathetic to Alexa's plight. She was the first one through, and she didn't stand a chance.

Here's the thing about parenting your firstborn: you think you know what you're doing, but you don't. You read a book, you watch some so-called parenting experts on TV, and you convince yourself you've got it all figured out. But then the reality of raising a tiny human smacks you in the face, and suddenly you realize you're just making it up as you go. And because you don't know any better, you go hard.

Alexa had to deal with peak, over-the-top, hyper-vigilant, no-nonsense parenting. There was no "let's see how this plays out" attitude. No sir. Every situation required action, a decision, a consequence. Bedtime was bedtime. Homework was not optional. Chores weren't up for negotiation. If Alexa stepped out of line, we corrected it. Immediately. Without hesitation. Without sugar-coating. Life doesn't hand out participation trophies, and neither do I.

Now, don't get me wrong—I love that kid. Love her to death. But part of that love is preparing her for the real world, not some fairy tale where feelings dictate reality. And she learned that fast.

Did she try to argue? Of course. Did she try to find loopholes? You bet. But being the oldest meant she had to deal with me at my most strict, my most unrelenting, and my most on-guard. She would later watch her younger sibling get away with stuff she never could, and I am sure she found it wildly unfair. And you know what? It was. But such is life.

That's the unspoken curse of being the firstborn—you get the parents when they still believe in rules. By the time Sophie, who is seven and a half years younger, came around, we had mellowed out a bit. Not because we cared less, but because we were just too damn tired. You fight every battle with the first one, but by the time you get to the last, you start picking your battles wisely. Plus, let's be honest, watching the first one screw up does wonders for the younger ones' decision-making skills.

At least, in theory.

But kids are dumb as rocks, so I'll probably get to repeat every single one of these lessons with Sophie. Lucky me.

Chapter 2 - The Sprite Can Test

So you think you're ready to be married? You think you're ready to have a family and love someone unconditionally? That's adorable. But let me ask you this—have you ever taken a partially full Sprite can to the back of the head, courtesy of a pissed-off toddler? Have you ever been screamed at by a three-year-old because you dared to swipe a single marshmallow charm from her cereal? No? Then you don't really know if you're ready for family life. Because parenting isn't all warm cuddles and adorable baby giggles. Sometimes, it's battlefield survival training, and your drill sergeant is three feet tall and fueled by sugar and unearned confidence.

One of the biggest lessons kids teach us—whether we want to learn it or not—is patience. And if you think you have patience now, congratulations on your blissful ignorance. Because nothing tests your resolve quite like a tiny human losing their ever-loving mind over absolutely nothing.

When I started dating Meg, her daughter Alexa was three. She was cute, shy, and understandably confused about the new guy in her house. She still saw her father occasionally, which only added to the complexity. Imagine being three years old and trying to figure out why all your friends at birthday parties have one dad, but you seem to have two. That's a lot for a kid. And to be fair, it's a lot for an adult too. It took me a while to grasp that she wasn't acting out because she was a "bad" kid—she was just trying to make sense of a world that didn't make sense to her.

That didn't mean it was easy. Or that I didn't get my ass handed to me from time to time. Like the time I stole a marshmallow charm from her cereal. Big mistake. Huge. I thought I was just teasing, being playful. She saw it as grand theft breakfast, and let me tell you, she was ready to take me to the highest court in the land. The meltdown was swift, brutal, and deeply humbling. Meg apologized on her behalf, but there was no taking it back. Alexa had won. I had been properly schooled in the laws of toddler justice.

And then there was The Sprite Incident.

Our first big trip as a makeshift family was a road trip in my RV—beaches, Knott's Berry Farm, and the Grand Canyon. We were making memories, or so I thought. Turns out, Alexa was making something else: a battle plan. After a long day at Knott's Berry Farm—one that already had its fair share of trauma—we were driving back to our RV, parked at one of our favorite spots, Dockweiler Beach in LA. The plan was simple: get dinner at Johnny Rockets on the Huntington Beach Pier. Solid plan. Reasonable plan. But we made one fatal error—we didn't consult the three-year-old.

Alexa had other ideas. Her favorite restaurant? Kentucky Fried Chicken. Specifically, the mac and cheese. And wouldn't you know it, we drove right past a KFC on the way to dinner. That was when all hell broke loose. She pleaded, she demanded, she wailed. And when words failed her, she went straight to the nuclear option: a half-full can of Sprite to the back of my head.

Now, let me be clear—I've been hit by worse. But a can of soda to the skull while driving is enough to make anyone reevaluate their life choices. Meg lost her mind. I, on the other hand, just sat there, head throbbing, in complete and utter clarity. Because in that moment, I knew. I was ready. I was ready to be a husband, a father, a punching bag for a tiny, confused human who didn't yet understand the world.

Love isn't just about the easy moments. It's about taking the hits and still showing up. It's about understanding that sometimes, a kid's world is so small that a missed mac and cheese opportunity feels like the end of it. There would be time for tough lessons. Time to teach her discipline and self-control. But that wasn't the moment. That moment was about patience.

Because love is patient. Even when it's wearing a Sprite can as a crown.

Chapter 3 - The Words You Do Not Say

There are plenty of things that fly in our house that might not in others. Cuss words? Sure, but with rules. We're not the kind of parents who sit around clutching pearls when a kid drops an F-bomb, especially when they're surrounded by grease, tools, and high-octane fuel in the race shop. It would be a little hypocritical for us to tell Alexa she couldn't swear when every third word out of our own mouths in that setting was "fuck." But that didn't mean she got free rein. No, those words had their place—race shop, race trailer, and nowhere else. And funny enough, she never really took advantage of it. Maybe it was too much power, or maybe she realized that just because you can say something doesn't mean you always should. The strongest words aren't the ones that come with four letters—they're the ones that shape who you are.

So, if "fuck" and "shit" weren't on the forbidden list, what was? There were three words in our house you didn't say. Words that, if you dared let them slip, had consequences. They were "want," "unfair," and "can't."

"Want"

Ever seen a kid in a store demand, "I want this!" and watched their exhausted parent cave to keep the peace? I see it all the time, and every single time, my reaction is the same: *no one gives a fuck what you want.*

When a kid says "I want," what they're really saying is "I am entitled to this." And that's not a mindset we were going to allow in our house. My own mother made sure of that when I was young. She had a saying: "Want in one hand and shit in the other—see which one fills up first." I can count on one hand the number of times I heard my mother swear, so when she did, you *listened.* And she was right. You don't get things because you *want* them. You get things because you *earn* them.

In our house, saying "I want" meant you *didn't* get. Period. If our girls wanted something, they had to ask with humility. "May I please have…?" That was the only acceptable way to make a request. And let me tell you, it stuck. Every friend who came along on vacations or family trips learned quickly that "want" was a fast track to *not getting a damn thing.*

"Unfair"

"That's unfair!"

Oh, really? You know what's actually unfair? Kids who go to bed hungry. Kids who don't have a home. Kids who live in war zones, wondering if tonight's the night their world gets blown apart. *That's* unfair. You getting told "no" when you ask for something? That's just life.

We drilled this into our kids early, and when Alexa had the audacity to tell us something was unfair, we made the penalty crystal clear: you can have whatever it is when you can afford to buy it yourself. Simple. Fair. And effective. Because life doesn't hand you things just because you think you deserve them. It hands you what you work for.

"Can't"

Of all the words we don't allow, this one is the worst. "Can't" is poison. "Can't" kills dreams before they even have a chance to breathe. "Can't" is an excuse wrapped in a lie.

A mentor on mine, Roger Lorenzini, told me something that stuck: "Can't never did nothing." Sure, it's grammatically challenged, but it's the damn truth. The moment you let "can't" slip into your vocabulary, you've already lost.

Sophie is a perfect example of this. If you ask her if she can throw a 60 mph fastball, she won't say "I can't." She'll say, "Not yet." That little shift in mindset is everything. There was a time when she couldn't even break 50. Then she did. Now she's at 59. And 60? It's coming. Because she knows "can't" isn't allowed.

Now, we're not unreasonable. "Can't" has its place in absolutes. "I can't wear size 6 shoes"—sure, the kid has flippers for feet, that's just reality. But when it comes to things within your power? *You damn well can.*

Walking the Talk

This isn't just about the kids. Meg and I hold ourselves to the same standard. And there's nothing better than when we slip up and Alexa or Sophie call *us* out. It means the lesson stuck. They understand the power of words and why we don't let these three into our vocabulary. They know that "want" breeds entitlement, "unfair" breeds self-pity, and "can't" breeds failure.

At the end of the day, I don't care if my kids cuss. I care that they are strong, capable, and humble. I care that they don't whine about what they think they deserve, but instead go out and earn it. And if that means dropping a well-timed "fuck" while tightening a bolt in the race shop? So be it.

Chapter 4 - The Two Words That Matter Most

So, we've just reviewed the words that aren't welcome in our home—the ones that make me raise an eyebrow, stop a conversation dead in its tracks, or maybe even send a shoe flying across the room. But now, let's talk about the words that *must* be spoken.

And no, I'm not talking about some fancy, high-society nonsense. I'm talking about two words that, if left unsaid, will set off something close to a firestorm in my house. (Okay, maybe not a *real* firestorm, but trust me, you'll wish it was.)

Those words? "Please" and "Thank You."

These aren't just polite little phrases to sprinkle into a conversation when you feel like it. These words are the foundation of respect, gratitude, and basic human decency. I'd go so far as to say they're the two most important words in the English language.

Now, I know there's some parenting trend out there that says forcing kids to say these things is somehow oppressive. That it should be their choice. That we shouldn't force them to express gratitude if they don't feel it. Well, to that I say, bullshit.

Manners aren't about feelings; they're about discipline and habit. They're about recognizing that the world doesn't revolve around you and that other people matter. You don't get a choice about whether or not you treat others with respect. It's a non-negotiable. In my house, "please" and "thank you" aren't optional—they are the price of admission to being part of the human race.

Alexa and Sophie have had this drilled into their heads from the moment they could talk. If they ask for something, they say "please." If they receive something, no matter how small, they say "thank you." No exceptions. I don't care if it's the waiter at a restaurant, a teacher handing back a test, or a stranger holding the door open. These words come out of their mouths automatically.

Why? Because I've made it clear that failing to use these words is unacceptable. If my kids ever barked an order at a server like some entitled little prince or princess, we'd be leaving the restaurant hungry. If they failed to thank someone who gave them a gift or a favor, they'd be writing an apology note before bedtime. And if they ever, *ever* acted like they were too important to use basic manners, we'd have a long conversation about humility that they wouldn't soon forget.

Here's the thing: life is hard. People aren't going to hand you things just because you exist. The world doesn't owe you kindness. But if you show respect and appreciation, you'll find that people are more willing to help you, give you opportunities, and show you respect in return. That's what I desire for my kids—the ability to build real relationships based on gratitude and respect.

At the end of the day, I know my kids will stumble. They'll make mistakes. They'll get things wrong. But if the one thing they carry forward from my parenting is that "please" and "thank you" matter—if they instinctively show appreciation and respect without me hovering over them—then I'll know I did my job.

And if there are any other words that should fall into this category, I'm all ears. But I have a feeling that if kids these days just mastered these two, we'd all be in a much better place.

Chapter 5 - The Lost Art of Saying No

Look, I get it—saying "no" is tough. We want our kids to be happy, to have what they want, to experience as much joy as possible. But if you think parenting is about making your kid happy 24/7, you're setting them up for a world of disappointment. The fact is, if you look at your own life, you've heard "no" more times than you've heard "yes." That's reality. And the sooner we teach our kids to deal with that, the better off they'll be.

Think about it. Salespeople get hundreds—maybe thousands—of "no's" before they get a "yes." Ballplayers? They fail 70% of the time at the plate, and that still makes them some of the best in the game. Looking for a prom date? Rejection after rejection before (hopefully) a victory. Life is full of "no." It's what we do after hearing it that defines us.

So why do parents today struggle with this simple, single-syllable word? Have we become so worried about our kids' feelings that we've forgotten to prepare them for reality? If you never say "no" to your kid, congratulations—you're raising a person who will crumble the first time life doesn't go their way.

With my daughter, Alexa, I made "no" my go-to answer. Even for things I was eventually going to say yes to, the first response was always "no." Why? Because I wanted her to understand that "no" is not an absolute—it's a starting point. It's a challenge. It's an opportunity to prove why she deserves a "yes." This wasn't about being cruel; it was about teaching perseverance. She learned quickly that "no" didn't mean the world was ending—it meant she had to work for it.

In business, I've always believed there are two types of people: "yes" people and "no" people. "Yes" people are the ones who make things happen, who push forward, who find a way. "No" people are the ones who always have a reason why something can't be done. And you know what? I love "no" people, because when they give me all the reasons something is impossible, they're handing me the roadmap to making it happen.

That's what I hope for Alexa. When she hears "no" see it as a temporary obstacle, not a permanent roadblock. She can learn to get comfortable with rejection, so she'd learn how to push through it. Because life isn't about how many times you get told "yes"—it's about how many times you get told "no" and still find a way to win.

Parents today need to stop being afraid of "no." Stop worrying that it'll crush your kid's spirit. If anything, it builds them up. If they get used to hearing "yes" all the time, they're going to grow up thinking life is easy, and when the real world smacks them in the face with a big, fat "no," they won't know what to do. But if they've learned that "no" is just part of the game, they'll keep swinging, keep trying, and keep pushing forward.

Saying "no" isn't about being mean—it's about being real. It's about teaching your kids that life isn't always going to hand them what they want on a silver platter. If they want something, they need to work for it. And if we don't teach them that now, the world is going to do it later—and trust me, the world isn't nearly as gentle as a parent who loves them enough to say "no."

So, do your kids a favor. Get comfortable with "no." Use it often. Make them earn their "yes." Because the strongest, most successful people in this world are the ones who didn't let "no" stop them—they used it as fuel to find a way to turn it into "yes."

Chapter 6 - The Art of Discipline

So, how does an old-school parent discipline their children? I know that's the burning question in all your minds. And I'll tell you right now—it's not what you think. Discipline isn't about breaking spirits; it's about building resilience.

Let's get this out of the way first: I believe in consequences. I believe in an eye for an eye. If thieves lost hands when they stole, we wouldn't need three-strike laws. But I can count on one hand the number of times my girls got a spanking. Not because I'm against corporal punishment—I'm not—but because discipline is about effectiveness, not theatrics.

Growing up, my dad's belt and my backside were well-acquainted, and let me tell you—I earned every one of those whippings. But raising girls was different. Maybe it's the dynamic, maybe it's just instinct, but I found that a well-placed punishment that targeted their priorities was far more effective than swinging a belt.

Take Alexa, for example. When she was little, the worst thing we could do was send her to her room. Now, that never made sense to me—her room was practically a toy store. Stuffed animals, books, dolls—you name it. The only thing missing was a pony, because we weren't idiots. But for some reason, isolation hit her harder than any spanking ever could. She craved connection, so removing it was the ultimate consequence.

Meg figured that out, not me. And it worked—until, of course, the cell phone came into play.

Unlike her younger sister, Alexa didn't get an iPhone until she was a freshman in high school. And that was the beginning of the great divide. She'd come home, head straight upstairs, and disappear into the digital abyss. We'd see her for a quick dinner, then she'd vanish again, "SnapTexting" or "InstaTweeting" or whatever the hell they were doing back then.

And that's when I discovered the ultimate parental weapon: taking away the cell phone.

Forget grounding. Forget extra chores. Forget even food rations—because I'm telling you, nothing, and I mean NOTHING, is more devastating to a modern teenager than losing that damn phone.

You think I'm exaggerating? I'd bet both my girls would have gladly signed up for a weekly ass-whooping if it meant keeping their phone.

There is no greater punishment in the history of parenting. If you want to see true despair, don't hit them—just take the phone. It's like cutting off their oxygen supply.

Now, this makes me wonder—when my girls have kids of their own, what's going to be the equivalent? Are we going to have to threaten to turn off their neural implants? Block their access to whatever virtual nonsense exists in the future? Who knows? But I'll tell you one thing—discipline will always come down to the same principle: Find what they value most, and use it to remind them who's in charge.

Raise kids who understand consequences, or prepare to watch them crumble at the first sign of adversity. Your choice.

Chapter 7 - Know When to Let Go

Every parent wants to share their hobbies with their kids. It's natural. You love something, you put your time, money, and soul into it, and you want your kid to experience that same passion. But here's the hard truth: just because you love it doesn't mean they will.

From the moment Alexa met me, I was a racer. It was in my DNA. I had raced everything from BMX bikes to offshore powerboats, and I was damn good at it. Alexa, my stepdaughter, had a wild streak. She wasn't one to take the easy way down an inflatable slide—nope, she'd rather launch herself from the top and see what happened. So, when she had been to enough races by the time she turned five, I figured it was time. That Christmas, Santa (with some financial backing from yours truly) brought her a kid kart. A proper 50cc Comer engine kart, the same thing all the other five-to-eight-year-olds were racing.

On Christmas morning, she was pumped. Sat in the seat, pushed the pedals, pretended to drive. She was excited, and so was I. Meg, had convinced me to dial the throttle back a bit for safety, and I am glad I did. It was winter, so the first real opportunity to drive didn't come until March when we got invited to my buddy James' birthday at Thunderhill Raceway. Perfect. I loaded up the RV, hitched up the trailer, packed my Lotus Exige and Alexa's kart, and we hit the road.

Now, the drive up should have been a hint at how the day would go. I got popped for speeding on I-5. The RV was way too powerful, and on those long, straight stretches, I was flying. The cop wasn't amused when I told him he was making me late for a race. Lucky for me, Alexa slept through the whole thing—also lucky the officer didn't ask to check the back, where my five-year-old was snoozing on the bed instead of being properly buckled in.

Meg wasn't with us that day—she had to work—so it was just me and Alexa. Fortunately, James' mom, Linda, was there. She adored Alexa and kept an eye on her while I hit the track. The Lotus was on fire that day, carving up Porsche GT3s like they were standing still. It was everything I loved about racing—speed, control, precision. But the highlight of the day, at least in my mind, was still coming: Alexa's big moment.

We went over everything. Left foot brake, right foot gas. We practiced in the paddock. She was suited up—full race suit, Simpson helmet, gloves—the kid looked like a pro. Then, it was go time.

Now, they say no plan survives first contact. That was painfully true that day. The second that little Comer engine fired up, Alexa went full send. She mashed the throttle like John Force at a drag strip. I could tell immediately that she was panicked, but instead of lifting, she did what every racer at heart does: when in doubt, throttle out.

The problem? She was aimed straight at the RV.

I took off running like my life depended on it—because in a way, it did. All I could think about was the conversation I'd have to have with Meg. "Hey honey, how's your day? Oh, mine? Well, funny thing happened at the track—I killed our kid." Nope. Not happening.

By some miracle, Alexa made a tiny adjustment, just enough for me to dive and grab the back of the kart. It started dragging me, but I managed to reach over and hit the kill switch. Silence. Relief. She was in tears. Terrified. And all I could do was hug her.

We loaded up the kart. She never drove it again.

As much as I wanted her to love racing, it wasn't for her. And that's okay. She tried BMX too, gave it a shot, had a massive yard sale wipeout, and that was that. By the time she turned sixteen, she was smart enough to say no when I offered to teach her to fly—because, yeah, I'm a pilot too.

Sometimes, our hobbies are just that—ours. It doesn't mean our kids will love them the way we do, and we sure as hell can't force it. What we can do is support them in finding their own thing. And when they do, we show up, we cheer them on, and we back them up just like we would if it were our own passion.

That's how you raise tough kids—not by forcing them into what you love, but by letting them figure out what lights them up and standing behind them every step of the way.

Chapter 8 - The Greatest Gift You Can Give Your Child - Confidence

Let's be honest—life isn't a damn fairy tale, and school is a war zone. We're taking our beloved, innocent child and tossing them into one of the most savage environments imaginable at the ripe old age of five (maybe earlier if you were crazy enough to send them to preschool). School is survival of the fittest, from kindergarten all the way through high school. By college, most kids figure it out—except for the Neanderthals, but that's not our concern. The best thing we can do as parents is prepare our kids for the battlefield. And the single greatest gift we can give them? Confidence.

Not the "everyone gets a participation trophy" kind of confidence. Not the "you're special because I said so" nonsense. I'm talking about the real kind. The kind that makes them walk into any room, stand tall, and know they can handle whatever gets thrown their way. And how do you do that? Glad you asked. The answer is simple—martial arts.

Stop Coddling, Start Training

Listen up, because this might hurt some feelings (not that I care). Stop taking your princess to dance class where she's taught to prance around like a damn circus performer for your entertainment. This does nothing—NOTHING—to build true confidence. If you're a "Dance Mom," you're part of the problem. If you're a father who lets his little girl spend her time twirling instead of learning how to throw a solid punch, you've failed her. Period.

Confidence doesn't come from putting on makeup and pretending to be something you're not. It comes from knowing—deep in your bones—that you can handle yourself. That if push comes to shove, you won't back down. And you get that through discipline, training, and knowing what it feels like to get knocked on your ass and get back up.

Nick's Story: From Nerd to Warrior

This isn't about Alexa—that's the next chapter. This is about Nick.

Nick started Taekwondo as a high school freshman. He was awkward, a classic nerd. Slumped shoulders, head down, barely spoke above a whisper. No eye contact. The kind of kid you just knew got overlooked, pushed around, or ignored.

Enter Mister Frega.

Mister Frega was their Taekwondo instructor, a multi-time national champion who maybe weighed 160 pounds soaking wet, but could knock you flat on your back before you even knew what hit you. I watched him at a tournament once—spinning hook kick to his opponent's head a few seconds into the match. The guy dropped like a tree, out cold. That's the kind of guy who teaches real confidence. Not some after-school counselor telling your kid to "believe in themselves." No, Mister Frega made them earn it.

Nick trained under him, day after day. And over time, something amazing happened. He stopped slouching. His head came up. He started making eye contact. He spoke louder. You could see the transformation happening in real time. By the time he and Alexa earned their black belts, Nick was a different person. Strong. Focused. Unshakable.

Then came Meg. When she started Taekwondo, she worked her way up, too. Eventually, all three of them were in the same black belt class. And you know what she told me? She hated sparring with Nick. Why? Because, in her words, "he's scary."

Damn right, he was. Because by then, Nick wasn't just a nerd. He was a fighter. And more than that—he had confidence. Real confidence. The kind you don't fake. The kind that lasts a lifetime.

"We Are No Longer Afraid"

At some point during this journey, I asked Nick, "How has Taekwondo changed your life?"

He looked me dead in the eye and said, "Mr. Young, I'm a nerd. My friends are nerds. We used to be scared to even go to lunch. We are not scared anymore. No one at school can hit me as hard as Mister Frega has, so if I can survive that, they cannot hurt me or my friends. We are no longer afraid."

Tell me—what greater gift can you give your child than that?

So, do the right thing. Get your kid in martial arts. Teach them to fight. Teach them to stand tall. Life isn't easy, and it sure as hell isn't fair. But a kid with confidence? They can handle anything. And that, my friends, is how you set them up for success. If every parent took this advice, there would be no bullies, think about that.

Chapter 9 - Too Much, Too Soon

Parenting isn't about keeping them comfortable. It's about pushing them—sometimes shoving them—toward their potential. But, as I learned the hard way, there's a line, and if you cross it, you might just push them right out the door.

Alexa's journey in Taekwondo started as a glorified playdate. She was a preschooler with some visual-spatial challenges, and Taekwondo helped her rewire her brain in ways I don't fully understand but will always be grateful for. What started as an activity with her friends quickly turned into something more. She wasn't the best in Poomsae—hell, I'd say she was average—but put her in a sparring match, and something inside her flipped. The more she got hit, the stronger she became. It was like watching a machine wake up.

At eight years old, she started competing in tournaments, and it was clear she had the mindset of a warrior. She stood her ground, took her hits, and delivered them right back—gold medal after gold medal. While her best friend dominated in Poomsae, Alexa owned sparring, the real competition.

Then came Reno. The UWTA National Championships. She fought her way through, knocking off a reigning champion from her own dojo in the semifinals. I remember watching the father of that girl lose his mind, berating his daughter for losing. It was a lesson in what not to do. You don't crush your kids after a loss—you let them feel it, process it, and get back in the ring. That poor girl? We never saw her again. Either they left or she quit. Either way, it was a waste of talent.

Alexa made it to the finals. Her opponent, Faith, was a literal giant compared to her. In Taekwondo, size matters. A longer reach means more power, more control, more everything. But Alexa wasn't fazed. It was David versus Goliath, and damn if David didn't come out on top. When that final whistle blew, Alexa was a national champion at nine years old.

That should have been the moment we let her breathe, let her enjoy what she had accomplished. Instead, the whispers started. People who knew the sport saw something in her. She had the "it" factor. There was talk of international tournaments—Australia, Korea, Europe. Bigger stages. Bigger stakes. The Olympic pipeline. And we were all in. What we didn't see was that she was only nine.

We signed her up for the USA Taekwondo National Championships. I should've seen the signs. She hesitated. She pushed back. Instead of backing off, I signed myself up too, thinking if I did it with her, it would help.

San Jose. The biggest stage we'd ever been on. The energy was electric, and Alexa had a target on her back. Everyone was talking about some girl from Miami, the one to beat. When the two finally met in the semifinals, Alexa cracked. Before the match, she was in tears. Not because she was scared of the fighter—Alexa never feared an opponent—but because she was afraid of failing, of letting us down.

She fought through it, round after round, tied after the first, ahead after the second. Her opponent's corner was in shock. Their fighter had never been down before. But in that tiny 30-second break, the pressure crushed Alexa again. More tears. More doubt. And by the end, she lost by just a couple of points. She finished third, earned a podium spot, and received offers to train with Olympic-level coaches. But none of that mattered.

We had broken her. We had put too much weight on her tiny shoulders. She wasn't afraid of fighting—she was afraid of disappointing us.

She went to one more tournament after that, and it was like watching a different kid. She lost every match to kids she could've beaten in her sleep. She was done. She made it crystal clear. She was nine years old, and she had already had enough.

People ask me if I think Alexa could've been an Olympian. Without a doubt. She had the heart, the skill, and the fight. But not at nine. The road to greatness is long, and we tried to sprint it in toddler shoes.

So, here's the lesson, folks: Push your kids. Teach them grit. Toughen them up. But don't be an idiot like I was. Recognize when they need space. Don't let your ambition—or anyone else's—drown out their voice. They'll tell you when they're ready, and if you listen, they might just surprise you with what they can do on their own terms.

Chapter 10 - Pets, Playdough, and the Lie Your Kids Tell You

If you don't have pets in your home, you're failing your kids. That's not an opinion; that's a fact. Pets teach kids some of life's most important lessons—love, loyalty, and the inevitable gut punch of loss. They also teach kids that responsibility isn't just something they can promise with a smile and a head nod—it's something they will eventually learn the hard way, whether they like it or not.

Now, let me be clear: Do not get a pet because your kid says they'll take care of it. That's a damn lie. They don't know it's a lie, but let's remember—these are the same humans who used to (or still do) eat Play-Doh. They have no real sense of cause and effect. They'll swear up and down that they'll feed, water, and clean up after their new furry friend, but I promise you, you will be the one picking up poop at 6 a.m. while they sleep through their "chores."

In our house, Meg ends up taking care of the animals. This isn't new. It started right after we got married when we brought home two French Bulldogs, Chapman and Elise. Chapman was the chillest dog I've ever known—he was my kind of pet. Elise, on the other hand, was an absolute spaz. When our daughter Sophie was

40

born, Chapman appointed himself her protector, mostly from Elise, who was always one tail wag away from a disaster. We had to say "No Elise" so many times that for a while, Sophie actually thought her name was "NoEz."

They were with us for 13 years. And when Chapman died, it hit our family like a freight train. Alexa and I went to see him one last time at the vet, and we just stood there and cried like a couple of babies. And then, because life doesn't pull its punches, Elise followed soon after. The second loss didn't make the first any easier—it just doubled down on the hurt. But that's the deal when you love something. Hazel, our Basset Hound, grieved right alongside us. She had spent her entire life with them, and even though she had no words for it, we could see it in her.

Did this emotional trauma make us wise enough to resist adding more animals to our home? Of course not. We're suckers, especially when our daughters put on a presentation like a couple of Disney executives pitching a new franchise. Case in point: the hamster debacle. Alexa wanted a hamster. A hamster. Absolutely not. No way in hell was our house going to host a rodent in a cage. But because I believe in making responsible parenting decisions, I countered with an alternative that made perfect sense to me: miniature Texas Longhorns.

Yes, cows.

Here's how that worked out: I found some mini Longhorns in Texas (naturally), and there was a truck in Houston I had been looking at, so I figured I'd kill two birds with one stone. The plan? Fly to Texas, buy the truck, drive to Dallas, pick up a trailer, grab the cows, and head back to California. Simple, right?

Wrong.

I had somehow forgotten that Meg grew up in the suburbs of LA and San Francisco, meaning her cowboy experience was zero. She spent the entire trip worried about the cows. I must have said, "Honey, they're fine" at least a thousand times, but she didn't believe me. She was convinced that every bump in the road meant they were being tossed around like lottery balls. Meanwhile, my truck rode like a brick, so in reality, the cows were probably more comfortable than I was.

After three long days, we made it home to Shingle Springs, CA. That's when the real work started. Cows are not like dogs. You don't just let them out in the backyard and throw them a bone. We had to build fences, because our big steer, Gunsmoke, kept breaking out. We lived in an equestrian community, and let me tell you—nothing pisses off fancy horse people quite like a Longhorn wandering down their pristine riding trails. I thought it was funny. They did not.

Then came building the housing. By "we," I mean me. Looking back, I'll admit: It probably would have been easier to just let Alexa have the damn hamster. But I wanted my kids to understand animals in a way that books and road trips past a cow pasture couldn't teach them. These Longhorns weren't just livestock; they were part of our family. Even Meg, my suburban girl who thought cows were just big dogs, fell in love with them—especially Gunsmoke.

When we moved to Kansas City, we couldn't take the cows with us, so they stayed with my parents until they couldn't care for them anymore. Letting them go was hard, but that's life. You take care of something, you love it, and eventually, you have to say goodbye.

The girls learned a lot from those cows. They learned that responsibility isn't just a promise—it's action. They learned that animals, even the biggest and toughest, need care and patience.

And they learned that loss never gets easier, no matter how many times you go through it.

Hopefully, someday, my daughters will pass these same lessons on to their own families. And when life throws them a challenge—whether it's a dumb cow breaking through a fence or something much bigger—they'll know they can handle it.

So, yeah. Get your kids a pet. Just don't buy their BS about doing all the work.

Chapter 11 - The Participation Trophy

When we first moved to Kansas City, we had a hell of a time finding a good soccer program for Alexa, who had just turned 12. Somehow, we ended up on a team called the Dragons. That name alone should have been the first clue that this wasn't going to be the team for us.

Of course, the coach's daughter was the "star"—because that's how these things always go. Which, whatever, it's soccer, so who the fuck really cares? Alexa enjoyed playing, but let's be honest, she didn't love it. And this team? This team sucked. I'm not even sure if they ever won a game.

Alexa got stuck playing forward, even though her natural position was center mid (how the fuck do I even know the positions on a soccer field? Someone, please, shoot me). After every loss, the coach would give the same speech: "You guys tried hard, it was a good, close game." Except it wasn't good, and it sure as hell wasn't close. Even Meg got tired of hearing the same old "you tried hard and should feel good about yourselves" bullshit. No, they shouldn't. They just got their asses kicked, again, while half the team stood around watching the other team run circles around them.

Poor Alexa. She'd manage to pick up a goal or two per game, but that was about all the fight this team had. And then we got to the season-ending tournament.

The way these people talked about this tournament, you'd think they were headed to the damn World Cup. In reality, only three teams showed up. And guess what? We finished third. With an 0-2 record.

After the final loss, they lined the girls up and handed them all third-place trophies.

Are you fucking kidding me? They got rewarded for that?

I looked at Alexa, and she looked back at me with pure embarrassment in her eyes. Meanwhile, her teammates were jumping up and down, thrilled that they had finally won what was probably their first piece of hardware in their lives.

As we walked out of the complex, Alexa didn't say a word. She just marched right up to a trash can and threw the trophy where it belonged.

Her teammates gasped in horror. "What are you doing?" one of them asked.

Alexa didn't even hesitate. "I don't want a participation trophy."

Proud dad moment? Hell yes. She was 12, and she already got it. No kid of mine was going to be raised thinking you get a prize just for showing up.

Chapter 12 - The Disney Cruise

One day, Meg and I were out shopping—probably at Costco, because feeding a family takes bulk-level quantities of food. Upon arriving home, we were ambushed by Alexa and Sophie, our two little masterminds, who had put together a full-on presentation about why we should take a Disney Cruise. Now, I say "presentation" loosely because this thing made the one from *Step Brothers* for Prestige Worldwide look like a TED Talk. It was a mess—slides out of order, questionable logic, and about as much polish as a third-grader's science fair project.

But damn it, they put in effort. And in our moment of weakness, Meg and I—seasoned Disney veterans who had done both Land and World—thought, *Sure, why not? How bad could it be?*

What the fuck were we thinking?

A Disney Cruise is next-level insanity. I mean, we knew Disney was a well-oiled machine of corporate magic and overpriced happiness, but this was something else. The pools? Forget it. Small, overcrowded, and basically a full-contact sport. You weren't just swimming in urine—you were getting kidney shots from kids and accidental elbows from overzealous dads trying to relive their high school water polo days. Meg and I took one look, got in for about three seconds, and then decided the only safe place was somewhere that served alcohol.

Then there were the Disney moms. If you think dance moms are intense, let me introduce you to the species known as *Disney Cruise Moms*. These women were up at 5:00 a.m. to reserve pool chairs like it was the Oklahoma Land Rush. They strategized like generals on D-Day to get their kids the best seats for whatever character meet-and-greet was happening that day. The sheer dedication was equal parts impressive and horrifying.

And let's talk about what was supposed to be *the best day* of the cruise—Castaway Cay, Disney's private island. Yeah, it rained. Not a drizzle, not a light, romantic mist. Full-blown torrential downpour. You haven't lived until you've seen grown adults, who paid thousands for this experience, standing in rain ponchos, forcing their kids to build sandcastles in the mud while pretending they're still having the time of their lives.

Now, for the real highlight of the trip—Alexa taking a spinning back fist to the nose. Now, before anyone calls CPS, let me explain. Alexa and I used to spar. Light contact, no real damage, just our thing. Meg hated it with the fire of a thousand suns, and on a cruise ship, in close quarters, her tolerance was even lower than usual (and her usual was zero).

So, there we are, in our cramped little cabin, and I go to execute a spinning backhand—totally controlled, I knew exactly where to stop. Except, you know, spinning attacks have that split second where you lose sight of your opponent. Alexa, thinking she'd be slick, decided to run past it and dodge. Miscalculated. BAM. Right in the nose. Blood everywhere.

Meg? Livid. Me? Horrified (but also a little impressed with the execution). Alexa? Just standing there, bleeding. Sophie? Probably saying something like, "She deserved it."

Moral of the story? I don't know, take your pick:

1. If you're going to be dumb, you better be tough.
2. A Disney Cruise sucks so bad that getting punched in the face was the highlight.

You decide. But I'll tell you this—we sure as hell aren't going on another cruise.

Chapter 13 - The Starburst Revolution

Kids need to learn hard lessons. It's better they learn them young and with candy than when they're older and it's their paycheck on the line. The world isn't fair, and no amount of coddling will change that. The sooner they figure this out, the better prepared they'll be to navigate life without crumbling under the weight of reality.

Alexa is a great kid, but school wasn't exactly her strong suit. So when she came home one day, practically glowing with pride, I knew something special had happened. Turns out, they played some kind of educational game in class where winners earned Starbursts. And for once, Alexa was on a roll. She was stacking up Starbursts like a Vegas high roller hitting blackjack after blackjack. I was thrilled. A win is a win, and in our house, we celebrate those.

But then came the twist—the teacher imposed a tax. And not just any tax, mind you. A tax *only* on the winners. Losers? They got to keep their empty hands in their pockets. Alexa, on the other hand, had to cough up her hard-earned Starbursts. She was livid.

"What kind of nonsense is this?" she asked me.

The answer was simple: it was a political science lesson. The teacher wanted the class to experience wealth redistribution firsthand. The winners were taxed, and the proceeds were handed out to those who didn't earn them. A classic lesson in how the system works for some and against others.

Now, I'm all for a little real-world education. But there's a fine line between teaching and indoctrination. The teacher thought she was imparting a valuable lesson in fairness, but all she really did was turn my daughter into a Republican faster than a year of Fox News in the background. When Alexa asked which party supports higher taxes, the teacher told her it was the Democrats. Alexa then asked what the other option was.

"Republicans," the teacher replied.

And that was that. Without hesitation, Alexa declared, "Then I'm a Republican."

I couldn't help but laugh. The irony was too good. A liberal teacher, probably thinking she was shaping young minds toward her own ideology, ended up teaching my kid a lifelong lesson in hard work, effort, and the reality of taxation. I would've sent the teacher a thank-you card if I wasn't sure it'd end up in the recycling bin next to her soy latte cup.

Of course, not every kid in that class learned the same lesson. Some probably walked away thinking, *Hey, if I don't try, I still get candy!* And that, my friends, is how you end up with a generation that believes handouts are a career path.

But for Alexa, the lesson stuck. She now understands that effort should be rewarded, not penalized. That success isn't something to be ashamed of. That life is about what you put into it, not what you can take from others. And that sometimes, the biggest life lessons come from the most unexpected places.

So, if you're worried about your kids falling for the soft, whiny, "life should be fair" nonsense, don't stress too much. Sometimes, even the most liberal of teachers can give your kid the wake-up call they need. Just make sure you're there to help them connect the dots. Because the world isn't about feelings—it's about reality. And the sooner they grasp that, the better off they'll be.

Chapter 14 - The Ring Doorbell Blockade

Ah, the first date. A milestone for every kid, a moment of reckoning for every parent. Alexa, my little girl—who was no longer quite so little—was heading out for her first official date with Perry, her Air Force Junior ROTC buddy. Now, let's get one thing straight: I liked Perry. He was a good kid. Always had a smile, respectful, and had that discipline that comes with ROTC. But that didn't mean I was about to let my guard down.

Meg and I had big plans that night ourselves—Queen with Adam Lambert. And yeah, yeah, I know, he's not Freddie Mercury. No shit. But the guy can sing, and it was still a hell of a show.

Before we left, Perry and his mom pulled up to take Alexa out. Meg was doing the polite mom thing, talking with his mother, while I handled the more important duty of issuing a firm yet loving warning. "Just remember," I told Alexa, "I'll be watching the Ring camera when you get home." Now, I didn't give a damn if they kissed or not, but I wanted her to know Big Brother was watching. It's a little thing called psychological warfare—one of a dad's greatest weapons.

Fast forward to later that night. There I am, enjoying the hell out of some live Queen, when my phone buzzes with a motion notification from the Ring cam. Oh, this is going to be good. Sure enough, Alexa and Perry were back. And then came the magic moment.

The kid thought he had a shot. You could see it in his body language—he was lining up for the kill shot, about to go in for the big moment. But my girl? She remembered my words. She executed what we now affectionately refer to as "The Butt Hug."

Picture this: Perry leans in, eyes locked, heart pounding, aiming for that first kiss. And Alexa? She leads with the butt, stepping back like she's evading a linebacker. Poor Perry doesn't know what hit him. He's got his arms out, ready to embrace, but she's already moving in the opposite direction. The result? Possibly the most awkward first-date goodbye in the history of young love.

And I? I was the man who cock-blocked a teenage boy using a Ring doorbell. That, my friends, is a dad win of epic proportions. Did I mention we have the video? Because you bet your ass we do.

But here's where life throws a punch to the gut. Perry, that sweet, polite, respectful kid, didn't get to live out his full story. When he was a freshman in college, he made the heartbreaking decision to end his own life. It devastated Alexa. They had remained friends long after their breakup, and he was still a part of our family's world.

I'll always remember Perry as the kid who did things the right way. He showed respect. He treated Alexa well. Even after they parted ways, he was the kind of person who could still come over, hang with the AFJROTC crew, and swim in our pool like nothing had changed. That's rare. That's real.

The world got a little darker the day he decided to leave it. But in our home, in our memories, we'll always have Perry. And I'll always have the satisfaction of knowing that for one brief, hilarious moment, I outmaneuvered a teenage boy with the power of technology and fatherly paranoia.

Rest easy, Perry. You were one of the good ones.

Chapter 15 - First Weekend Driving; Lies, Deception, and a Bent Bumper

There's something about your kid getting their driver's license that makes you question all of your life choices. Maybe it's the realization that the same child who once ate Play-Doh and thought they could fly off the couch with a blanket cape is now in control of a 3,500-pound death machine. That'll sober you up real quick. But hey, we're old school—trial by fire, right? So when Alexa got her license, we didn't hold her back. We handed her the keys to her brand-new Jeep Wrangler Willys 2-Door and let her loose.

Now, before anyone starts clutching their pearls about a 16-year-old getting a brand-new car, let's be real. My girls are spoiled. I own it. But let's not pretend this Jeep was some kind of luxury vehicle—it had manual locks, crank windows, and no heated seats. That's about as close to roughing it as a new car gets. Plus, it was built to last, which we knew would come in handy because teenagers and sound decision-making rarely go hand in hand.

So, the first weekend arrives, and Alexa, in a moment of big sister generosity, offers to take her 8-year-old sister Sophie out for the day—lunch and the mall, a classic bonding adventure.

Meanwhile, Meg and I had our own plans: "Front Nine and Wine," a golf tournament where the main goal is to drink progressively more at each hole and somehow make it back to the clubhouse without losing a shoe or a marriage.

Everything was going fine until they got home. And by "fine," I mean Alexa had wrecked the Jeep.

Five. Damn. Days. Five days into having her license, and the Jeep already looked like it had seen battle. The front bumper was pushed back and up on the passenger side—nothing catastrophic, but still enough to make me want to bang my head against a wall.

Then came the story.

According to Alexa, she had parked at the mall, gone inside, and when she came back out, someone had hit her car and fled the scene. Now, I've been going to that mall for years. Never once has anyone hit my car. But suddenly, five days into driving, she's the victim of a hit-and-run? Yeah, okay.

Now, here's the thing—I knew she was full of it. So did Meg. But I had an ace up my sleeve: Sophie.

Sophie is my girl. She's loyal—to a point. And that point is when she thinks she can earn brownie points with Daddy. So when she backed up Alexa's story, I'll admit, I was momentarily thrown. Maybe, just maybe, my kid was telling the truth?

Nah. Not buying it.

Enter my genius parenting move of the night.

We were golfing with my buddy Jeff, who owns a good-sized security company in the KC metro area. Before we left, I looked Alexa dead in the eye and said, "Good news! Rockwell Security does the surveillance for that mall, so I'll have Jeff's guys pull the footage. We'll find out who hit your car and go after them."

I saw it immediately—the sheer panic in her face. Eyes wide. Color draining. I swear I saw a tear start to form. It was beautiful. Meg and I then promptly left to go drink wine and forget about the whole thing for a while.

Six hours later after we returned from our night out, I'm in my office when I hear whispering outside the door. Alexa is confessing to Meg. I hear Meg say, "Well, you need to go tell him." That's when I knew—I had her.

Sure enough, Alexa slinks into my office and comes clean. Turns out, she wasn't even at the mall. She had been at Panera, misjudged a parking spot, and hit a parked car. My first thought?

"Why the hell were you at Panera? You're 16. Go to Chipotle like a normal teenager. Panera is for suburban moms and retirees."

The punishment? No insurance claim—she was going to fix the Jeep herself. This is why we got her a Wrangler. It's basically a Lego set for grown-ups. But honestly, the real punishment was the six hours she spent thinking she was about to get exposed on security footage.

Then came Sophie. My sweet, loyal, totally full-of-it daughter who had backed up Alexa's nonsense. I headed to her room, where she had shut the door and was crying. That kind of thing rips a dad's heart out, but I had to stay strong. If she sensed weakness, she'd own me for life.

The second I walked in, she blurted out, "Daddy, I will never lie to you again, I am so sorry! Alexa promised to take me shopping at Claire's!"

Bribery. Classic. Honestly, I was kind of impressed Alexa managed to get her on board.

But the lesson had to be learned. After a bit of a lecture, she went to bed.

The takeaway? My kids now know we're always two steps ahead. They learned that lies have a way of unraveling, that I have an imaginary army of security cameras at my disposal, and most importantly, that no matter how smart they think they are, we're smarter. Have they lied since then? Probably. But I guarantee every time they do, there's a little voice in their head wondering if I already know.

Chapter 16 - Lessons in Metal and Grit

There's a certain satisfaction in watching your kid tackle a challenge head-on, armed with a little guidance and a lot of grit. It's a lost art these days—raising kids who can handle themselves without falling apart at the first sign of adversity. That's why, after Alexa had a little fender bender in her Jeep, I didn't rush to coddle her or call the insurance company. Nope, this was a teachable moment, and by God, we were going to make the most of it.

Once the dust settled and we had a chance to survey the damage, we found it was all cosmetic. The front bumper had taken the brunt of the hit, but luckily for Alexa, that just meant an opportunity to upgrade. Jeep folks love a good excuse to modify, and this was the perfect time to introduce her to the world of practical problem-solving. After a quick search on Amazon, I found a kit that would allow us to turn the damaged bumper into a "stubby" style—shorter, cleaner, and way better for rock crawling… or, in her case, curb climbing.

A few days later, the parts arrived, and it was time to get to work. We headed to my shop, where I house and work on my race cars, a place filled with enough tools to build a small tank. I laid out everything she'd need: a

Sawzall, files, a drill, wrenches—everything necessary to get this job done. We marked the bumper with blue painter's tape to give her a cutting guide, and after a quick rundown of what needed to happen, it was go time.

Alexa grabbed that Sawzall with the determination of a kid who's about to learn a valuable life lesson the hard way. She fired it up and dug in like a tick on a bloodhound. Progress was slow, painfully slow. Every few minutes, she'd stop to check the blade, squint at the bumper, and then go back to sawing. A job that should have taken five minutes on both sides turned into a 30-minute war between my daughter and a hunk of metal. The cuts looked like a blind surgeon had performed an amputation—jagged, uneven, and generally a mess. She finally stopped, looked at me, and asked what she needed to do.

Being the "World's Best Dad" (as confirmed by a mug Sophie gave me for Christmas), I decided to step in. One glance at the Sawzall and I had my answer: she was using a wood-cutting blade. No wonder she was struggling. I walked over, swapped it out for a metal-cutting blade, and went to work. That new blade sliced through the bumper like a hot knife through butter. Alexa stood there, jaw on the floor.

"Why was it so easy for you?" she asked, still in shock.

I tossed her the old blade. "Read the side."

She looked at it. In big red letters: "WOOD."

"And what does that mean?" I asked.

"It's for wood," she mumbled.

"Exactly. Today's lesson: know your tools. Work smarter, not harder. I mean, I love hard work—I could watch it all day long. But there's no point in struggling when the right tool makes all the difference."

With that lesson learned, we moved on, cleaned up the cuts, and bolted on the new end caps. Within 20 minutes, the job was done, and honestly, the bumper looked better than when it rolled off the assembly line. Great job, Alexa.

That one little project was just the beginning. Since then, she's learned how to change her oil, rotate her tires, and when we bought some jet skis, she installed a hitch receiver all by herself. Most recently, she even swapped out her own brake pads. And guess what? She did a damn good job.

Most parents today would have taken their kid's car to the shop and paid a mechanic to do the work. But what lesson does that teach? That money solves all problems? That you should just hand over your hard-earned cash instead of learning how to handle things yourself? Not in my house. At least now, if she decides to pay someone to change her oil, she understands the value of the work and the money she's spending. And that's the kind of knowledge that sticks with you for life.

The world needs kids who know how to handle themselves, figure things out, and get the job done—even if it means making a few rough cuts along the way.

Chapter 17 - Flying Under the Radar is for Cowards

One night, we were at a restaurant having a nice family dinner—well, as nice as a dinner can be with my crew. I have no idea how the conversation took this particular left turn, but at some point, my daughter Alexa dropped a bombshell. She said her strategy in high school was to "fly under the radar." No waves, no standing out, just blending in and existing.

Meg and I were appalled. I mean, what in the actual hell? That is *not* how you go through life. You don't just float along like some anonymous face in the crowd. You get out there, grab life by the throat, and punch it in the damn mouth. You take chances, make mistakes, and let people know you exist. You do *not* just "be."

At that moment, the conversation shifted to cars (as things often do in our house), and Alexa said she loved her Jeep because it was white and "blended in." The rage that filled my soul was almost indescribable. My daughter—a product of *my* household—was openly advocating for being vanilla, invisible, a background character in her own story.

At that point, things probably got a little loud.

We began brainstorming how to "fix" this nonsense, because in our family, we don't do boring. In my infinite wisdom, I declared that she was going to drive something that could never fly under the radar. Something that made a damn statement. Something like a Lotus.

Alexa balked, of course. She argued that there was no way she was driving a Lotus to school. And my response? "The hell you won't, we are getting a Lotus and you *will* drive it."

The people in the booth next to us must have thought we were fucking insane. But this is Missouri, where no one drives foreign sports cars, so we already stood out like sore thumbs. Might as well lean into it.

Then Sophie, chimed in with, "I want a Lamborghini."

Oh, for the love of God.

That was a hard *no.* The last thing Sophie needed was *more* attention. She had no problem making a spectacle of herself already. She was getting a damn Toyota Camry—reliable, boring, and about as flashy as a church pew.

But the Lotus? That was happening.

So, I got to work. It didn't take me long to track down the perfect 2011 Lotus Evora in California. Had a buddy—who owns Lambos, so obviously a trusted source—check it out. He told me it was perfect and that if I didn't buy it, *he* was going to. Well, that sealed the deal. Next thing I knew, I was booking a flight to California to pick it up.

I won't bore you with the logistics of getting that beast back to Kansas City, but let's just say it was a process. A fun, exhilarating, absolutely-worth-it process. There was only one small problem: in my fervor to teach my daughter about making a statement, I had overlooked one crucial parenting detail.

I had forgotten to teach her to drive a stick.

I tried. Lord knows I tried. But let's be honest—some people are just not meant to drive a manual transmission, and Alexa was one of them. That, my friends, was yet another *parenting fail* on my record.

So here's the thing—there's no real profound lesson in all of this, except maybe that I managed to turn a dinner conversation about "blending in" into getting myself a Lotus.

Alexa has *never* driven that car. Not once.

But do I care? Absolutely not. Because at the end of the day, there's nothing quite like ripping around town in a street-legal go-kart, reminding everyone that life is too damn short to fly under the radar.

Mission accomplished.

Chapter 18 - Lessons through Fireball

There comes a time in every parent's life when you see that glimmer in your kid's eyes—the moment they start wondering about the forbidden. For Alexa, it was Fireball. And for me, it was a chance to prove that good parenting isn't about bubble-wrapping your kid. It's about teaching them the right lessons, the right way, at the right time.

We were at a buddy's house, taking celebratory shots every time the Chiefs scored, which felt like every 30 seconds in the Patrick Mahomes era. That's when I caught Alexa's curious gaze. I wasn't naïve—I knew exactly what she was thinking.

Now, some parents would have shut it down immediately. Some would have launched into a lecture about the evils of underage drinking, grounding their kid into the next century if they even touched the bottle. But that's not me. I don't believe in pretending the real world doesn't exist. The question isn't whether your kid is ever going to take a sip of alcohol—it's whether you've raised them with enough sense to know when to say no and when to walk away.

I wasn't about to hand her the bottle, but I also wasn't going to pretend she wasn't going to drink at some point in her life. So, I let her have a sip.

And let me tell you—it did not go well for her. The sweet cinnamon taste gave her just enough confidence to swallow, but the burn that followed made sure she learned her first drinking lesson the hard way. Her face said it all: Dr. Pepper tastes a hell of a lot better than Fireball.

That moment didn't turn her into a raging alcoholic, and it sure didn't make her reckless. If anything, it demystified alcohol for her. We had already done the work—we had shared stories about people we knew who had died because of drunk driving. She had never seen her mother or me get blackout drunk, and she sure as hell never saw us get behind the wheel after drinking. She learned by watching, not just listening, because kids pay more attention to what you do than what you say.

Fast forward to her high school years. We had this amazing industrial refrigerator in our basement living area—the kind you see behind a bar. The left side was fully stocked with beer, seltzers, white wine, Mikes Hard Lemonade—you get the picture. And guess what? We never locked it. Not once did I come down in the morning after a swim party and find the fridge raided. If something was missing, it was maybe a beer or two from the back—just enough for some high school kid to think they were getting away with something, but not enough to do real damage.

Now, could I have been wrong? Could I have missed something? Maybe. But I raised Alexa to respect limits. I raised her to understand that just because something is there doesn't mean you need to abuse it.

As for Fireball and Alexa, well, college brought its own set of learning curves. I've heard she had a few encounters with it that didn't go in her favor. So when I ordered a round of Fireball shots for my 59th birthday, the horror in her eyes was all the confirmation I needed. She downed it like a champ, but I know damn well she won't be raiding my stash any time soon. My fifth of Fireball in the freezer is still safe—at least for now.

The point is this—raising kids isn't about keeping them away from everything. It's about preparing them for it. The world isn't a padded playground; it's full of hard lessons. Our job isn't to shelter them—it's to make sure they can handle those lessons when they come. And if that means letting them take a sip of Fireball under your watch instead of sneaking it at some house party with God-knows-who, then so be it. That's called parenting.

Chapter 19 - Leadership, Grit, and a Dirty Swimming Pool

There are two kinds of people in this world: those who rise to the occasion and those who sit in the corner whining about how hard life is. In this family, we raise the first kind. If you want something, you better be willing to fight for it. That's the lesson Alexa learned between her junior and senior year of high school when she attended the JROTC leadership training at Camp Clark in Nevada, Missouri.

Alexa was pumped. This wasn't just some summer camp where kids sit around a fire singing Kumbaya. This was the real deal—a week of military-style training designed to toughen up the next generation of leaders. Cadets from all over Missouri would be attending, and Alexa was ready to prove herself.

Now, let's talk about Camp Clark. This wasn't some posh, state-of-the-art facility with air conditioning and spa amenities. This was an old Missouri National Guard base that hadn't seen an upgrade since the Cold War. The barracks were raw—beds lined up military-style, no privacy, no fluff. The swimming pool looked like a science experiment gone wrong, full of algae and questionable life forms. And hot water? Forget about it.

Meg, ever the trooper, volunteered as a chaperone, meaning she got to bunk in the barracks right alongside Alexa and the cadets. But Meg is no fool—she also booked herself a room at the local Holiday Inn for those moments when a real bed, a hot shower, and a little sanity were needed. Can't say I blame her. If there's one thing I've learned in marriage, it's that tactical retreats are a sign of intelligence, not weakness.

The week was intense. The cadets were pushed to their limits, physically and mentally. They had to work together, overcome obstacles, and prove they had the grit and resilience to lead. It was exactly the kind of experience that separates the wheat from the chaff.

On graduation day, Sophie and I hopped in the Lotus and made the quick drive down to Camp Clark to witness the closing ceremonies. When we arrived, it was obvious—Alexa had been through the wringer. She looked exhausted, but there was fire in her eyes, that telltale sign that she had faced down challenges and come out stronger. Meg, on the other hand, looked fresh as a daisy, like she had just enjoyed a nice hot shower at the Holiday Inn. Go figure.

The ceremony was filled with speeches and awards, but then a commander from a Kansas

City inner-city JROTC program stepped up to speak. This guy was a chiseled, battle-hardened badass. You could tell just by looking at him that he had been through hell and back, probably more times than he could count. The second he opened his mouth, the entire room locked in. He was the kind of leader whose presence alone demanded respect.

He started by recognizing the top-performing team, a group of boys who had dominated the combat obstacle course. They were fast, strong, and efficient, everything you'd expect from a winning squad. But then, instead of stepping down, he kept talking. He had one more story to tell.

This wasn't about the fastest team. This was about a group of girls who had struggled their way through, fighting for every inch of progress. They weren't first, hell, they may have even been last, but there was one cadet who refused to let her team fail. She finished the course, turned around, and saw her teammates struggling. Without hesitation, she ran back into the chaos to help them push forward. She didn't care about her own success—she cared about the team.

And that, according to this hardened military leader, was what real leadership looked like. Not strength. Not speed. But heart.

"This cadet exemplifies what it means to be a soldier," he said. "She was without a doubt the finest cadet I saw all week. Not because she was the biggest. Not because she was the fastest. But because she cared more about her team than she did about herself. That is a true leader."

That cadet?

Alexa Holibaugh.

Damn right she was.

That moment right there is what this whole book is about. Raising kids who aren't afraid to get their hands dirty, who don't quit when things get tough, who understand that real success comes from lifting others up, not just pulling yourself ahead.

So, if you're wondering what it takes to not raise a snowflake, take notes. You push your kids to be tougher than the world that's waiting for them. You teach them that life isn't fair, and that's not an excuse—it's a challenge. You show them that respect is earned, not given, and that real leaders don't leave anyone behind.

And if they happen to get a little muddy, a little bruised, or a little worn down in the process? Good. That means you're doing it right.

Chapter 20 - Air Horns and F Bombs

Parenting isn't about making your kids' lives easy. It's about making them strong, resilient, and aware that actions have consequences. That's why, when I woke up one fine morning to find that my daughter's boyfriend had spent the night in my house, I knew it was time for some old-school, no-nonsense parenting.

Now, don't get me wrong—I love my daughter, Alexa. She's a good kid. But being a good kid doesn't exempt you from facing reality. And in my house, reality comes with accountability—and sometimes an air horn.

The night before, Alexa had a sleepover with her two friends, Krystal and Bailey. They were watching movies downstairs in our game room, enjoying the massive 80-inch TV I worked my ass off to afford. I could hear them laughing when my wife and I went to bed. No big deal—typical teenage fun. But when I woke up the next morning, something was off. I noticed a pair of unfamiliar size-15 clodhoppers sitting by my front door. Then I looked outside and saw a truck that hadn't moved since the night before.

This didn't add up.

After confirming with my wife that, yes, the truck still being there meant Ben, Alexa's boyfriend, was still in the house, I decided it was time for a wake-up call. Literally. I walked into my office and grabbed a trusty little air horn. You know, the kind people use at sporting events or to scare off unwanted intruders? Turns out, it works just as well on teenage linemen who don't understand household boundaries.

When I stepped into the game room, I saw Krystal already awake, trying not to laugh. She knew what was coming. On the far side of the sectional, there was Ben, a 6'3", 270-pound high school tackle, blissfully unaware that his morning was about to take a turn. On the closer side of the couch, Alexa was still sound asleep, oblivious to the impending storm.

I didn't hesitate.

BLAAT!

The sound echoed through the room like a foghorn on a battleship. Ben's eyes shot open, and for a split second, I swear he defied gravity. Alexa bolted upright, looking horrified. Meanwhile, Krystal lost all composure and burst into laughter.

Ben scrambled to his feet, his massive frame wobbling like a drunken sailor in a hurricane. That's when I asked the question that any father in my position would have demanded:

"What the fuck are you doing here?"

Now, let's get one thing straight—I wasn't *accusing* him of anything inappropriate. But the fact remained that my daughter's boyfriend had fallen asleep in my house, and I sure as hell wasn't about to let that slide.

Ben looked like a deer in headlights, struggling to find words as he tried to regain his bearings. He started looking around for his shoes, which was when I added,

"Please tell me your truck wouldn't start, because that's the *only* fucking reason you should still be here."

No response. Just more fumbling and stammering.

By the time he found his shoes and made his way to the door, he was practically tripping over himself. I turned to Alexa and said, "You better go kiss him goodbye, because this might be the last time you see him for a while."

She didn't argue. Smart girl.

Suffice it to say, that was the *first and last* time we ever had a boyfriend sleep over. And you know what? I have no regrets. Some might call it over-the-top. I call it parenting. You don't raise strong kids by letting them do whatever they want. You raise strong kids by making damn sure they know the rules—and that those rules have teeth.

Ben learned a lesson that day. So did Alexa. And if I had to guess, so did every other boyfriend that ever stepped foot in my house after that.

Mission accomplished.

Chapter 21 - Tough Love and Life Lessons

Taking in a foreign exchange student was always something I had wanted to do, but Meg was a bit more hesitant. She's got the biggest heart in our family, but even she wasn't sure about the commitment. That all changed when the phone rang one day. There was a young lady from the Philippines who needed a home—her initial placement wasn't working out. The group coordinating the exchange reached out to us, and Meg, being who she is, stepped up without hesitation. And just like that, the wheels were in motion. Bedrooms were reassigned, adjustments were made, and we prepared to welcome a new family member.

I'll be honest—she wasn't exactly what I had envisioned. I had this grand idea that we'd get some sporty kid who'd blend right in, maybe someone who could kick a soccer ball around with Alexa. Instead, we got a girl who was into choir and theater. Theater. Seriously? Of all the things? I mean, couldn't she at least fake an interest in sports? But, as always, life has a way of giving you what you need rather than what you want.

She was a sweet kid, though. Tough in her own way. She came from a rough situation back home—her mom was Catholic, her dad was

Muslim, and she had grown up navigating both worlds. The pictures she shared of her home were eye-opening. The poverty she had endured was humbling, to say the least. Coming to the U.S. was a world of excess for her, and I can only imagine how overwhelming it must have been.

It wasn't an easy year. Communication was tough, not because she was difficult, but because she didn't want to be a burden. That meant we often found out about things at the last minute, scrambling to make adjustments. But we made it work. We took her on trips to LA (Disneyland, of course), Las Vegas (because, well, Sin City is a sight to see), and New York. We even took her skiing in Tahoe, and let's just say, that was a challenge. The cold, the unfamiliarity, the frustration—she wanted to quit about five minutes in. But quitting wasn't an option in our house. She kept at it, and by the end of the trip, she was getting by just fine on the bunny hill. It wasn't graceful, but it was effort, and that's what mattered.

As the year came to an end, emotions ran high. Graduation day was supposed to be a celebration, but Alexa was sulking. She was consumed with the fact that she wouldn't be the first in our family to graduate high school. Are you kidding me? This girl who had come from nothing was living her dream, and all Alexa could think about was herself? It was disappointing, and while we never really tackled that head-on, I like to think karma stepped in to handle it for us.

Fast forward to 2020. Alexa's senior year. COVID-19 had other plans. Senior prom? Nope. Traditional graduation in May? Not happening. Instead, her graduation was pushed to July and held at the Sporting KC soccer complex. And in that moment, I hope she realized something—being the second to graduate in our family didn't make her any less important. She was still our number one.

Life has a way of teaching lessons whether we're ready for them or not. Tough love isn't about being mean—it's about making sure kids understand that the world doesn't owe them anything. Our foreign exchange student got that. She appreciated every opportunity because she had seen what life was like without them. Alexa? She had to learn it the hard way. And sometimes, that's just how it goes.

In the end, we sent our exchange student back home with a huge care package filled with things for her and her family. She and the girls still stay in touch, and I hope that friendship lasts a lifetime. But more importantly, I hope both my daughters learned something from that year—that life isn't always fair, but how you handle it is what matters.

Chapter 22 - Choices Have Consequences, and That's a Damn Good Thing

When we sent Alexa off to college, there was one rule: don't screw it up. That's it. Simple, right? Well, as any parent knows, what seems simple to us is never quite that way for our kids.

Alexa started strong. She enrolled at the University of Central Missouri, joined ROTC, and got a taste of military life without signing her soul over to Uncle Sam. Smart move. She wasn't quite ready for full-time duty but loved the structure and discipline. That first semester, she had an opportunity to join a National Guard program that allowed her to serve part-time while staying in school. It was a win-win: keep her GPA up, stay in the program, and keep moving toward her goals. Everything was smooth sailing—until she joined a sorority.

Now, let me be clear. I don't have a problem with sororities, but I do have a problem with letting fun get in the way of responsibility. Alexa had always been a straight-laced kid, never one to party in high school. She spent her weekends with her Air Force JROTC friends, and their idea of cutting loose was maybe hitting up an ice cream shop. But college? Different ballgame. She jumped headfirst into the social scene—lake trips, parties, the whole nine yards. And just like that, school took a backseat.

As parents, we want our kids to enjoy college, to grow into who they are, but we also want them to remember why they're there in the first place. When Alexa's GPA tanked below the required 2.5, she got booted from the officer program. And here's the kicker—since she was already in the Guard, that meant one thing: boot camp. No cushy officer route anymore. She had signed up, made a commitment, and now she had to pay the price.

And that, folks, is how life works. Choices have consequences. You screw up, you don't get a free pass. You deal with it, you own it, and you move forward. No crying, no excuses. That's how you build character.

So, on a dreary day in Missouri, we drove our little girl—our sorority-loving, social butterfly—to the Guard base in Clinton. From there, she shipped off to Fort Sill for training. Back in the day, when a kid went to boot camp, you didn't hear from them until they were done. But times change. Alexa got one quick call to let us know she made it. Then silence. For weeks. And when that first Sunday call came? She sounded great—better than great. She was thriving.

Every week, the calls came, and she was more excited than the last. She told us about throwing grenades, qualifying with her rifle (which she already knew inside and out because we built an AR-15 together), and even handling the gas chamber like a champ. Apparently, one in sixty blonde women are immune to the effects of tear gas—who knew? While everyone else was gagging and crying, she stood there wondering when the drill was going to start. That's my girl.

By the time graduation rolled around, Alexa wasn't just surviving boot camp—she was leading. She was recognized as a top performer among hundreds of cadets, proving once again that when she sets her mind to something, there's no stopping her.

Life isn't about making perfect choices—it's about handling the consequences when things don't go as planned. And Alexa? She handled it. She manned up, did the work, and came out stronger on the other side.

If you want your kids to be tough, let them fail. Let them struggle. And most importantly, make sure they know that when they make a commitment, they damn well better follow through. Because when they do, they won't just survive life—they'll own it.

Chapter 23 - Music & Mayhem

Let me just say this up front: music matters. What your kids listen to will absolutely shape how they think, how they feel, how they act, and in some cases, how much therapy they'll need when they grow up. If you think it's just "background noise," you're either deaf, naive, or both. Music gets inside a kid's head faster than any lecture you'll ever give. Trust me—I've raised two daughters and survived the full gauntlet from Barney to Taylor Swift. Barely.

Now, if you're raising daughters like I am, then God help you. You've likely been sentenced to a lifetime in Swiftie hell. Don't get me wrong, Taylor is talented. She can write a damn good song. But after the fifteenth time hearing her whine about the latest breakup, I'd rather pour bleach in my ears than hear *All Too Well* one more time.

Fortunately, there's light at the end of that tunnel. My girls, Sophie and Alexa eventually found their way to country music—real country. We're talking Morgan Wallen, Megan Moroney, Lainey Wilson, Hardy, Luke Combs... hell, even a little Reba and Alan Jackson thrown in for good measure. That's what I call *acceptable indoctrination*.

See, my house wasn't built on lullabies and nursery rhymes. It was built on Buck Owens, Glen Campbell, Tanya Tucker, and the lyrical wizardry of Roger Whittaker. (Yes, I know, Roger isn't exactly "country," but that man could whistle your soul clean.) My dad played his music like it was gospel. You couldn't escape it, and honestly, I didn't want to. That's where my foundation was laid.

Then came high school. Hair bands. Big hair, bigger guitars. Bon Jovi. Poison. Mötley Crüe. Throw in some Hank Jr. and it was like my own coming-of-age soundtrack. Hell, when Hank released *Young Country*, I thought he had been watching my life like some outlaw version of The Truman Show.

Now fast forward to when Meg and I were raising the girls. While most people were playing *Baby Shark*, we were blasting Disturbed. Yep. You read that right. *Down with the Sickness* and *The Sound of Silence* were part of their bedtime routine. Maybe a little twisted? Sure. But the truth is, Disturbed's music, for all its aggression, has depth. It's raw but not reckless. It's heavy, but not hateful. It's music with a message—just delivered through a sledgehammer.

We even made a family memory out of it. A few years back, we bought meet-and-greet tickets for a Disturbed concert in St. Louis. Sophie and Alexa came with us. That year's Christmas card? A family photo with the band. Most families send out pictures in matching pajamas. Ours featured a heavy metal backline. Merry Christmas, ya filthy animals.

As they've gotten older, the girls settled into their own groove. They still sing along when I crank up Alabama or Garth Brooks. We've built playlists together, gone to concerts together—yes, including Morgan Wallen and Hardy. These are family events now. And that's the point: music isn't just noise—it's a connection.

Parents, listen to me: you *can* influence your kids' tastes. Not by force, but by exposure. Don't hand over the AUX cord and disappear. Make music a family affair. Play the songs you love. Talk about why you love them. Let your kids share their stuff too. Even if it sucks, listen. Just maybe not in the car on a long road trip unless you enjoy slow, painful brain death.

Bottom line: music is a gateway. It opens doors to conversation, culture, values—and yes, even rebellion. Use it wisely. If you let TikTok and whatever degenerate playlist is trending on Spotify raise your kids, don't be surprised when they start dressing like a Hot Topic clearance bin and quoting Cardi B as gospel.

Instead, bring them up on music that means something. That hits the heart, even if it hits hard. Whether it's country, rock, or whatever the hell Disturbed is classified as—make sure it's part of your family story.

Because trust me, there's nothing sweeter than hearing your teenage daughter belt out "Friends in Low Places" from the back seat, while flipping through your playlist and skipping over Taylor Swift

Chapter 24 - The Next Chapter

Raising kids is about preparing them to handle the world as it is—not the sugar-coated, hand-holding version some people want it to be. And if there's one thing we know for damn sure, it's that Alexa is more than prepared. She's out there writing her own story, and we wouldn't have it any other way.

Alexa is National Guard strong—one weekend a month, two weeks a year, plus whatever extra she signs up for because, let's be real, she's not the type to just sit back and do the bare minimum. She goes off to drill, where she gets to do all the things soft-handed people in this world would call "scary." Guns, big rigs, camping out in the elements—it's basically an action movie with a government paycheck.

The rest of the time? She's grinding. Two jobs, making ends meet, and living on her own. No safety nets, no handouts—just grit, independence, and the will to make it happen. That's how you raise someone who doesn't crumble when life gets tough. We taught her early that life if you want something, you work for it. And guess what? She listened.

Now, if she's got a guy in her life, well, I'll know when it matters. She's smart enough not to bring home every random dude, and honestly, I respect that. When she does, though, I'll know in about two minutes if he's got what it takes. Let's just say, I'm a pretty good litmus test. If he can't handle me, he sure as hell isn't cut out for Alexa.

Meg and I are watching her future unfold with excitement, because we know our daughter. She craves adventure, thrives on challenges, and isn't built for a boring, predictable life. Some kids grow up wanting a white picket fence and a nine-to-five; Alexa is out there chasing something bigger. Maybe she'll take the long way around to get where she's going, but wherever she lands, she'll be a force to be reckoned with.

What we do know is that she is built to survive. Built to lead. Built to make a difference. We love you, Alexa, and we couldn't be prouder of the woman you've become. And while we support whatever path you choose, let's be honest—would you just go be a peace officer already? You were born for it, kid. Go protect the weak and keep the wolves in line.

We're watching. We're cheering. And we'll always be your biggest fans.

Conclusion

If after reading this book you wonder if I have a PhD or other advanced degree in child psychology, you are too stupid to have kids. Please head to your local veterinarian to be spayed or neutered. I have the only credentials that matter: firsthand experience. While the Alexa Experiment is a work in progress, the outcome looks damn good.

Raising kids isn't about feelings. It's about results. It's about taking those tiny, screaming, sticky-handed chaos machines and turning them into adults who can actually function in the real world—without whining, without expecting handouts, and without crumbling when life smacks them in the face.

The world is not soft. The world is not fair. And the world sure as hell doesn't care about your kid's self-esteem. But it does care whether or not they can work hard, take a punch, and get back up. That's what this book is about. Raising kids who aren't afraid to fail, who don't think "unfair" is an excuse, and who know that respect is earned—not demanded.

If that makes me old-school, good. If that makes me harsh, I don't give a damn. My kids are tough, smart, capable, and, most importantly, prepared for reality. They know how to handle themselves in a fight, they know how to work for what they want, and they sure as hell know not to expect an award just for showing up.

I wrote this book because somewhere along the way, parenting turned soft. Somewhere along the way, parents decided that making their kids comfortable was more important than making them strong. That's how we ended up with a generation that needs safe spaces when they hear an opinion they don't like. That's how we ended up with kids who expect success to be handed to them instead of earned. And that's exactly what needs to change.

So if you're still with me, if you've read through these pages and nodded your head instead of clutching your pearls, then congratulations—you're one of the few who still understands what parenting is supposed to be. You get it. You understand that love isn't about coddling. Love is about preparing your kids for the world they actually live in, not the one they wish they lived in.

It's about pushing them when they want to quit. It's about letting them fail so they can learn to get back up. It's about making them understand that life doesn't owe them a damn thing—but if they work hard, take responsibility, and toughen the hell up, they can earn everything.

This isn't just a book. It's a call to arms. A challenge to every parent who still believes in raising kids who can handle themselves. Because if we do our jobs right, our kids won't need safe spaces. They won't need handouts. They won't need anyone to protect them from life. They'll stand on their own two feet, ready to take on whatever the hell comes next.

So go on. Get out there and parent like you mean it. Raise kids who won't melt at the first sign of trouble. Raise kids who are built for the real world. Raise kids who don't need participation trophies—because they know how to win.

I hope you have enjoyed reading Air Horns and F-Bombs, The Alexa Experiment and hopefully had a few laughs on the way. Now we get to improve our parenting skills with our second child (who is a polar opposite from the first), all I have to say is…..

Sophie, you're on deck!

Made in the USA
Columbia, SC
28 May 2025